Finding Y.E.S.

Your Essential Self

Nea Anna Simone

Bespoke Media Publishing House

Finding Y.E.S.
Nea Anna Simone

© **2023 Bespoke Media Publishing House LTD.**

Published by:
Bespoke Media Publishing House LTD Atlanta, 30309, GA, USA
A CIP record for this book is available from the Library of Congress Cataloging-in-Publication Data

ISBN-13: 978-0-9858833-7-9

Printed in USA

Dedicated to my children

Endia

A'ja

&

Caramia

and grandchildren

Avian & Ahnix

For The Journey Between

No Longer

&

Not Yet...

Foreword

Each of us reading this book began our life journey before we were even consciously aware of it or understood what a journey meant. Even now, we are probably better equipped to describe a childhood adventure like treasure hunting, or digging a hole to China in the backyard, than to decipher that we in fact have begun our life's journey. Did you receive love, warmth, affection, and encouragement or did you wonder why it was so readily available to others and not to you? Did you wish for the television image of family to replace the emptiness you felt on this journey you hadn't realized you were to take alone?

Whether we were called by name, or out of our name, the too's.... Too fat, skinny, ugly, dumb, stringy hair, too curly, too nappy, too short...never enough. Never quite fitting in to the image you held as acceptable. It is these things that shape us and how we view ourselves and our journey.

This journey was shaped not only by our parents whose messages may have been mixed, or well-intentioned people who were in the midst of it all. Our journey began by distinguishing the sensation of touch. Was the touch we received warm and loving? Or was the touch from the hand of someone whose touch repelled or repulsed?

As we matured, we understood languages and words, but also learned the ability to communicate in other ways. We understood through experience that a look could speak volumes without articulating a word.

The journey that has shaped us began without our knowledge or our permission. We were molded by the way our parents, relatives, teachers, or schoolmates described us. Like osmosis we unconsciously assimilated to the names we were called; the acceptance that we did or didn't receive, shaped our journey and our self image long before we realized it. The fact that we believed that these people "really knew" us, reinforced our belief of their perception. We then drew unto ourselves to confirm the messages we clung to as our identity. Although we may have mentally or verbally rebuked the message, it had burrowed into our spirit and held like a tick.

More than what we've been taught, what we've been told about ourselves, has in many instances led the charge in our journey through life. For those of us that were able to overcome these private obstacles and turn them around, they still dangle at our feet, occasionally hitting against our ankle… Always an uncomfortable reminder, that spurs the whispers in our mind that tells us we're not enough. This was for many of us our first view of the things, the thoughts, and experiences that caused us to dwell in our valley. How did I get to this place?

I often wonder, and then I recall that I am the child who never understood or believed whispers of beauty or intellect. I vividly recall the taunts of lanky, odd, ugly, mixed up. So, although I had seen what love looked like in the eyes of my parents when they gazed upon each other in an unguarded moment. I would look at my mother and understand why my father fell hopelessly in love with her.

Everyone always exclaimed at my mother's beauty. But, when I would gaze in the mirror I saw this fraud that she had given birth to. I believed that in order to be adored you had to have something I didn't possess, beauty like my mother's. Although as I matured into womanhood I ignored the mirrors and would tell myself a different story. But in that secret suitcase that I had packed for my journey, I still recalled the scars left by words, the barbs, the descriptions. The memory was vivid even if the scars weren't visible, I believed they could still be seen upon close inspection.

For some, entering the valley occurred shortly after birth. Perhaps born without parents, born with a disease, a disability or other challenge. Others may have experienced valley conditions in childhood, in a family where an abused, or abusive parent was the norm; or molestation robbed them of their innocence.

The valley was there, the journey had begun, and some made it through to adulthood. Others may not have been aware valleys existed because of idyllic childhoods and were rocked to their core to experience the world first hand as an adult in all its cruelty.

Whatever your beginnings, your journey is to find Your Essential Self.

Just know it is still possible. Today, all you have to do is choose.

I did.

With Love for Y.E.S.

Nea Anna Simone

Contents

PART I

Riding The Waves

*"During each stage of our journey from
infancy to adulthood our ears and
emotions are simultaneously attuned
to the voices of our parents and peers
as the truth.*

*Like a computer program that works in the
background, it influences behaviors and decisions
without our awareness.*

*Many of us accepted the input and continue along
ignoring or medicating the gnawing dis-ease.*

*It is Time to stop swimming against the current
and choose Your voice. Ride the waves and listen
to Your Truth. Find Y.E.S."*

Nea Anna Simone

Thoughts

Meditations

Thoughts

Date

Meditations

Before Y.E.S

On your journey to Y.E.S
you must first be able to say
NO!
It is a full and complete statement...

Thoughts

Date

Meditations

Thoughts

Date

Meditations

No Explanation

If you don't have to explain
Why
you responded
Yes.

Then you should

never explain
Why
you responded

No!

Meditations

Thoughts

Date

Meditations

No Regrets

I don't mind Failing...

I don't like to fail

but

when I do

I dust off and start again.

I do mind Regret

because it means

I told myself

No

when it may have been a Yes...

Failing is not failure....

Regret on the other hand is....

Thoughts

Date

Meditations

Date

Meditations

Anticipation

I am no longer PUSHED by Pain....

I am PULLED by Spirit.....

I am no longer the expression of the
design and intent of others.

I am in the midst of
discovery of my soul intent.

My heart rejoices that
I am no longer
who I once was...
and
I anticipate unlocking the
treasures within.

Soon to come
but
Not Yet...

Meditations

Thoughts

Date

Meditations

Practice

....The Day I realized I
could not fail
because it was just practice...

I decided to walk barefoot
through the sand
and
ignore the Hits and Misses.

That was the day that life became Fun!

Thoughts

Date

Meditations

Thoughts

Date

Meditations

The Moment

Why wait?
for Joy
for Love
for Happiness
for Fulfillment

The moment.
This moment
is all you have.

Thoughts

Meditations

Thoughts

Meditations

Permitted

Do You!
Without apology
Without guilt
Without regret

Give yourself permission to
Be Bold
Be Happy
Be Sad
Be Silly
Be Quiet
Be Loud
Be Loving
Be Brave
Be Kind

BE YOU!

Thoughts

Meditations

Thoughts

Date

Meditations

Highways

A Highway is a methaphor for life.

There are two lanes.

One coming and one going.

One to give.

One to receive.

No matter how far you go in one direction,

life will alter the course and

the road you're traveling

will come to an end

and

a new road will appear taking

you in a new direction to

receive all that you given.

So make sure you have also Forgiven.

Thoughts

Meditations

Thoughts

Meditations

The Assignment

YOUR ASSIGNMENT

To identify
To acknowledge
To learn
To appreciate
To accept
To love

Then you will enter a
state of well being.
Then you will experience joy.
Then you will know true happiness.

Thoughts

Date

Meditations

Thoughts

Date
....

Meditations

Territory

Today I entered a new territory
and
I am amazed at the view.

Although I am unable to see every detail
or
anticipate the turns in the road,
I proceed with gratitude
and
anticipation of the
goodness that awaits me.

The chill from the valleys
are at my back
and
I no longer recall
the obstacles.

Spirit is my Guide.
Faith is my Ally.
Love is my Comfort.

Thoughts

Date

Meditations

Thoughts

Date

....

Meditations

The Stumble

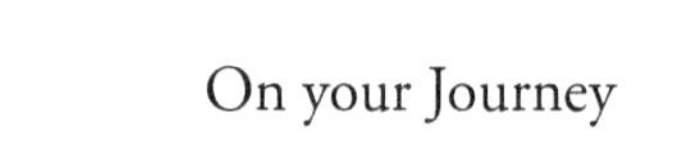

On your Journey
You may Stumble upon the Past...
You may Stumble upon People...
You may Stumble upon Opinions...

But eventually You will
Stumble upon Truth.
Then You will find Freedom
and
Step into Your Purpose.

Thoughts

Date

Meditations

Thoughts

Date

Meditations

Balance

It doesn't matter if the fog is thick or
the waves rough...
Stay focused...
Keep your balance...
Maintain confidence in your vision
And Stay the Course
Your destination to
sink, swim, or sail,
is your choice!

Thoughts

Meditations

Thoughts

Date

Meditations

Don't Should on You

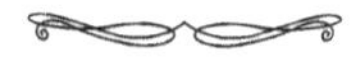

Whatever you do...
Don't SHOULD on
your dreams
your ideas
your goals
your life
Yourself!

Thoughts

Date

Meditations

Thoughts

Date

Meditations

PART II

Ripple Effects

"*You are a work of art!*
Like Michelangelo's "Creation of Adam",
which forms part of the Sistine Chapel's ceiling
or
Basquiat's "Pork", 1981,
the ultimate Artist ne Creator,
sculpted you to perfection!

You must believe this, even as you mentally review
all the reasons this statement is wrong…in your
heart of hearts at your deepest level there exists the
sense that I speak the truth of us all."

Nea Anna Simone

Thoughts

Meditations

Thoughts

Date

Meditations

Bad & Good

No matter what you've been told
You don't have to take the
Bad with the Good!

Why would you choose to
ignore the Bloom to
Focus on the Thorns?

Thoughts

Meditations

Thoughts

Meditations

Today

Move beyond Your obstacles.

Its NOT Faith,
if FEAR
stands in your way.

Thoughts

Date

Meditations

Thoughts

Meditations

Blocked

If
Obstacles
Adversity
Trials
&
Trauma
are your valleys.

Forgiveness is the mindset that will
diminish their effect and allow you to ascend.

Perseverance is the action to manifest
Opportunity
Advantages
Triumph
&
Testimony
to your mountain peak.

Forgive early
Forgive often.

Thoughts

Meditations

Thoughts

Meditations

Presents

So often we spend time
focused on
what passed in the Past

or Dreaming of
what may happen in the future

That we miss out on the
Presents
of
HIS Presence!

Thoughts

Meditations

Thoughts

Date

Meditations

Expect

Expectation!

The juncture
between where you are
and
where you want to be.

Where you Want to be, is your Desire.

Where you Are, is your Habit of Thought.

Focus on your want....

Envision your Desire
until your Habit falls away.

Thoughts

Date

Meditations

Thoughts

Meditations

Intertwined

Faith & Fear!

Intrinsically intertwined.

The one you choose will

navigate the terrain

to your destination.

Choose wisely!

Thoughts

Date

Meditations

Thoughts

Meditations

Lost & Found

Today

I lost my

History

&

Found

My Freedom!

Thoughts

Date

Meditations

Thoughts

Meditations

Storyteller

When you tell your story to others
Tell the story You Love!
Do not tell your story like a documentary
focused on traumas and tragedy.

Instead, tell the uplifting, fanciful stories of
your life....
the times that made you laugh,
or filled you with love,
and watch what happens.

It will feel like magic
as your life moves
on the wings of happiness and
love begins to transform
your experience.
But, it is not by magic,
but manifestation.

Speak life!
Speak joy!
Speak love!
And it will be yours!

Thoughts

Date

Meditations

Thoughts

Meditations

The Leader

Follow the leader when...
Love Leads the Way

Beauty Follows

Happiness Arrives

&

Joy leaves a Trail....

Thoughts

Date

Meditations

Thoughts

Date

Meditations

When...

When

Everything is Said & Done...

What have you really said or done?

Faith without Works
is only a
Wish!

Thoughts

Date

Meditations

Thoughts

Date

Meditations

Time...

Yesterday, did you
Wait
Watch
or
Act?

Today, did you
Wait
Watch
or
Act?

Tomorrow, will you
Wait
Watch
or
Act?

Thoughts

Date

Meditations

Thoughts

Meditations

GrateFUL

Explore

Embrace

Dream

Discover the gratitude of Love

that can only be Revealed

when it is Felt!

Thoughts

Date

Meditations

Thoughts

Date

Meditations

Repair

Hate for anyone
is
Hate for everyone
It is a double edged sword
wielded blindly.

Put the weapon away
Allow Love to enter
and repair the heart
disfigured by pain.

Thoughts

Date

Meditations

Thoughts

Meditations

The Ask

Isn't it funny how often in life
We ask for
and
even insist upon receiving
the very thing
that we are unwilling
or
unable to offer...

FORGIVENESS....

Thoughts

Date

Meditations

Thoughts

Date

Meditations

New

It is a New Day

As you imagine & verbalize
you New Story, your New Life.
Repeated often enough
You will believe it.

And when that happens
the evidence will flow quickly
into your experience.

A belief is only a thought you continue to think.
When your beliefs match your desires
they become your reality!

Be intentional....

Thoughts

Meditations

Thoughts

Meditations

Within

Look within...
Inspiration is there!

It is the light within you.

Inspiration is not Motivation.

Motivation is doing something
that you Must do.

Inspiration is allowing Spirit to be your Guide!

Thoughts

Meditations

Thoughts

Date

Meditations

Forgive

Anger
Pain
Hostility
Hatred
are self-imposed chains of bondage
that imprisons you from experiencing
Joy
Peace
Happiness
Love

Forgiveness is the key,
but only you can unlock the door
and set your Spirit free!

Thoughts

Date

Meditations

Thoughts

Date

Meditations

Unchanged

"Build Your Hopes on
Things Eternal.
Hold on to God's
Unchanging Hand."

Author: Jennie Wilson

The blessing of maturity lies not in material
possessions...
But in the Truth that God's Love is unchanging.
We are the ones who change.
This change is Always our choice.
Whether we choose:

Fear

Lack

Abandonment

Limitations

or

Love

Peace

Fulfillment

Abundance.

In both instances, God is there.

Thoughts

Date

Meditations

Thoughts

Date

Meditations

Free

Freedom is
the moment
you realize
you don't need permission
to fulfill your vision or mission.

Thoughts

Date

Meditations

Thoughts

Meditations

Y.E.S.

From the moment we can understand
most of us have been told and
have heard the word
No
more than we have
Yes.
No,
dangles in front of us
always within reach, while
Yes,
is often harder to find.
This NO training from infancy hardwires us
to expect a No
and never seek a Yes

Don't be afraid to find YES!

Thoughts

Date

Meditations

Thoughts

Meditations

The Mask

Take off the Mask!

Everytime you withhold yourself
by putting on a mask
or
allow others to diminish you.

You are intentionally
disregarding the Creators manual
and allowing the
Destruction
of your
Unique Design.

Date

Thoughts

Date

Meditations

PART III

Ebb & Flow

"Many of us reflect upon the happiest and most content moments in our life journey and our mind settles upon the times when we have been inspired enough to create. Whether we have created a good meal, work of art, a business, clothing or even another human being.... The act of creation is the most gratifying and lingering sense of accomplishment.

That is not to say that labor is not involved, obstacles, or frustrations as we strive to make our creation perfect. It is summed up in the fact that because we are inspired, it brings out the very best of our senses and heightens our ability to tap into a limitless reservoir."

Nea Anna Simone

Thoughts

Date

Meditations

Thoughts

Date

Meditations

The Stand

FEAR & FAITH
Will always be divided
Only You can decide
the side where
You will
Stand.

Thoughts

Meditations

Thoughts

Meditations

Show Your But...

Don't be Afraid to Show Your BUT...

Are you like a peacock strutting ...
feathers spread always on display?
OR
Are you the eagle who faces headwinds and
still seeks the mountain?

The peacock's beauty dazzles when they
show their butt.
But,
it is the eagle who endures
and
overcomes to achieve greatness
that we admire.

It is our shortcomings,
the obstacles,
The Buts
that make us better…
stronger...
that make us who we are
that are worth showing.

The Peacock
shows his butt,
while the
Eagle
Faces his Buts.

Thoughts

Meditations

Thoughts

Meditations

Sight

You have sole ownership and control of your vision.
The ability to manifest what you want lies
within you.
Don't muddy your vision with "reality"

Ignore what everyone else thinks
about what you want.

Your work is to clarify and focus
So that your vision becomes manifest reality!

Thoughts

Date

Meditations

Thoughts

Meditations

Worship

Creativity
is the purest form of
Worship.

It is the experience of
Allowing
Spirit
to flow
in and through
You!

Thoughts

Date

Meditations

Thoughts

Meditations

The Quest

How can you

Love

Honor

&

Respect

someone else

until

You

Love

Honor

&

Respect

Yourself!

Thoughts

Meditations

Thoughts

Meditations

Empathy

Empathy...
Pouring into others
until
their impotence
became evident
and
their needs endless....

Power...
When I stopped looking for vessels to fill
and
harnessed the
Potency
of my Faith
then I began to Create.

Thoughts

Meditations

Thoughts

Date

Meditations

Alchemy

Alchemy
The process of turning
Lead into Gold.

Alchemist
What I became
when I was
Led to my Goal.

Thoughts

Meditations

Thoughts

Date

Meditations

The Altar

Whatever you place on
the Altar
of Your heart
Will
Alter
Your Soul
with the Power
to
Brighten or Dim
The Light of Your
Spirit.

Thoughts

Date

Meditations

Thoughts

Meditations

Accept

To Receive
You Must Choose to
Accept

Either....

Dreams or Nightmares
Joy or Pain
Peace or Distress
Happiness or Sadness
Love or Hate

The Choice is Always Yours!

Thoughts

Meditations

Thoughts

Date

Meditations

Feelings

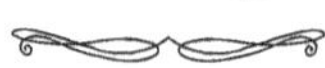

If you feel Joy
it is temporary.
&
If you feel Joyless
it is also only temporary.

Your present reality
is only an expression
of your past thoughts.

Now, Focus on What You Want
Not on What You Don't Want.

Thoughts

Date

Meditations

Thoughts

Meditations

Unfinished

With each new desire allowed to manifest
You will discover another desire

&

vision waiting to be expressed.

The process of manifestation
is not about finishing.

It is another opportunity
to expand creatively

and

enjoy the opportunity of
expansion and manifestation
to continue thriving.

Thoughts

Meditations

Thoughts

Meditations

Choose

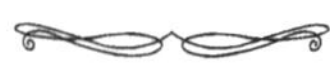

Everyone has the power to
direct the course of our lives
by choosing
what we will
&
won't do.

Although its easier to believe
we don't have this power to choose.

The truth is
the choice is always
Ours...

Thoughts

Meditations

Thoughts

Date

Meditations

PART IV

Following the Tides

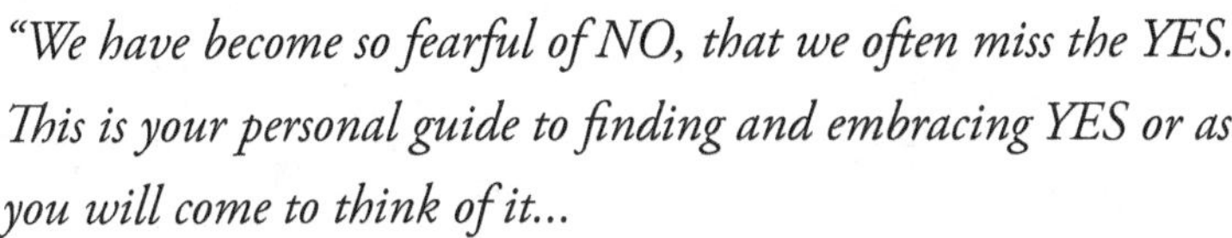

*"We have become so fearful of NO, that we often miss the YES.
This is your personal guide to finding and embracing YES or as
you will come to think of it...
Your Essential Self as a Guide preparing You For the Journey
Between No Longer & Not Yet."*

Nea Anna Simone

Thoughts

Date

Meditations

Thoughts

Date
....

Meditations

Focus

Focus helps us identify
the Desires of the Heart.

If you allow the Desires to Flow
You Thrive.

If you stop the Flow
You Survive.

Surviving is Not Thriving
Its Striving.

Allow the Flow of Creation
to Bring your Desires to
You.

Thoughts

Meditations

Thoughts

Meditations

EX-pression

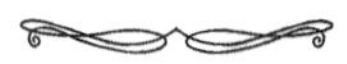

Yen and Yang...

Yen:

I didn't want You when I had You.

Yang:

Now I want You and can't have You.

Thoughts

Meditations

Thoughts

Meditations

Rejection

When I realized I will never be

younger

than I am at this moment

I ceased my fear of tomorrows

and

realized that

age and aging

is just an idea that

I had accepted

&

an outcome

that I had expected...

And then, I *rejected* it.

Thoughts

Meditations

Thoughts

Meditations

The Path

Grateful

That the Path ahead of me

is further than my eyes can see...

&

the road of my experiences

exceeds my ability to remember.

Thoughts

Meditations

Thoughts

Meditations

Truth

Only Ugly
when it is hidden.

Only Acceptable
when used to judge others.

Only Scary
when it means accepting change.

Only Hidden
from fear of consequences.

Only Freedom
when it is faced.

Thoughts

Meditations

Thoughts

Meditations

Differences

The Difference between a

Dreamer & Believer

is that while

the Dreamer dreams

the Believer concieves

&

expects to acheive and receive.

Therein lies the difference between

Manifestation & Hope.

Thoughts

Date

Meditations

Thoughts

Meditations

Faith is Action

I believed when I was Barren.

I believed when I was Full.

I moved in my Belief

Trusting

Despite the Reality

Despite Opinions

Despite Outcomes

Still I Believe!

Date

Thoughts

Meditations

Power

She understood being different was her power

So she moved to her own tempo

Created her own beat

And allowed the world to

Learn her rhythm.

Thoughts

Date

Meditations

Thoughts

Date

Meditations

Listen

When someone unknowingly touches you with
a message that resonates deeply
within your soul.

Recognize that
Spirit is Speaking by Proxy.

Lean in and listen carefully
for now you are hearing the Truth....

Thoughts

Date

Meditations

Thoughts

Meditations

Invitations

Stop sending mental invitations
to the unworthy to
offer opinions on your
vision and goals.

Free your mind
Focus only on what you want.
Not what someone
wants for you.

Thoughts

Meditations

Thoughts

Date

Meditations

Wandering or Wondering?

Wandering

is an aimless action

with an elusive destination.

It is the dwelling place of Procrastination

that jealously guards your focus from

progress.

Wondering

is a magnet for Creativity

allowing you to Manifest

Your Thoughts, Dreams & Visions

into Reality.

It is action incarnate!

Thoughts

Date

Meditations

Thoughts

Meditations

The Day

The day you realize your

Journey Will Never Truly End

is the Day

You experience true

Peace and Purpose

unencumbered by Fear.

Date

Meditations

Thoughts

Date

Meditations

Love

How Do You Define Your
Ability to Love?
Do you Say
"I can only Love this and Not That"
That is like saying
"I love the flower, but not the bud."

True love requires seeing
the object of your adoration
through the eyes of the Spirit.

Then even as the flower fades & withers
You witness the transition of each Petal
with Gratitude.

When true love exists
the bounty of your joy
is evident to all,
as love, like beauty,
cannot be denied once experienced.

Thoughts

Meditations

Thoughts

Date

Meditations

Age

....And the tree did not bow with age for

it understood that its strength

lay not in its branches, bloom,

or leaves,

but in its roots....

Thoughts

Date

Meditations

Thoughts

Meditations

Choice

Choice is a Super Power.
Don't hide your Strength under a
bushel and place the Choice
of Others
over Yours.

Choosing is the first step
There is no wrong choice
It is what You
choose to Do
After the choice
is Made...

Thoughts

Date

Meditations

Thoughts

Date

Meditations

Be Happy

I am an advocate of
Happiness!
Be as Happy as you can
and everything will take care of itself.

Even if you don't have a reason to be happy
make it up
fantasize it
Make a decision that
you're going to be happy
one way or another
No
Matter
what...

If you ignore negativity
and meditate on happiness
Make happiness your mantra
repeat
I'm Going to happy!
I'm Going to be Happy!
And You Will Experience Happiness!

Thoughts

Meditations

Thoughts

Date

Meditations

Bound

Holding a Grudge
binds & blinds you
to the possibility and experience
of
love
joy
peace
happiness

Free Yourself!
Take the blinders off
FORGIVE

Thoughts

Date

Meditations

Thoughts

Date

Meditations

Goodness

Use every moment
to find the Good that exists.

Dwell on the Good

Spend time thinking on it

Seek it out

The more You seek Good

The more God sees who
you are trying to Become...

Thoughts

Date

Meditations

Thoughts

Date

Meditations

Role Play

Victim...

Villian...

Victor...
You have played each role convincingly.

But remember it is only
role play.

You are Human, the writer, producer & director of
the role you choose and design.

Forgiveness will release you from the bondage of
role play to find your true self.

Thoughts

Date

Meditations

Thoughts

Meditations

But's

My BUT is bigger yours...
Bigger than your facts
Bigger than your version of my reality
Bigger than your denial of my possibilities
Because my But is followed by...
Faith
Determination
Hope, and
.....GOD....

Thoughts

Date

Meditations

Thoughts

Meditations

Decisions

I have never made a Good decision

and

I have never made a Bad decision.

I have made decisions

and

each decision

became a journey

where I learned

I can always

Decide!

Thoughts

Date
....

....

....

....

....

....

....

....

....

Meditations

....

....

....

....

....

Thoughts

Meditations

The First Time

The First Time I found Y.E.S. I was told I was too
young to know
and I believed it.

The Second Time I found Y.E.S I was told that I should be
more focused on the happiness of others
and I believed it.

The Third Time I found Y.E.S. I was mourning the loss of
my Could Have Been and
was told it was too late
I had missed my opportunity
and I believed it.

Ah... but the Fourth Time I looked past the passage
and saw myself and Y.E.S.
I ignored the voices from
within and without to concentrate on freeing the inner me
that had struggled to see the light............

Looking up I exhaled YES!

Thoughts

Meditations

Thoughts

Date

Meditations

Silence

Silence is often the most feared and desired
it is not only a state of mind,
but also a state of being
that allows presence of mind
and honest reflection.

Is silence your fuel or your fool?

Thoughts

Date

Meditations

Thoughts

Meditations

The Ending
&
The Beginning

"On the Journey Between
No Longer & Not Yet,
I hope you continue to
investigate, question,
learn & grow.
There is no destination to growth,
but self-acceptance is a destination...
You will arrive."

Nea Anna Simone

Thoughts

Date

Meditations

Thoughts

Meditations

A Good No

All No's aren't created equal!

Sometimes all you really need is
A Good No, to help you
Find Y.E.S.

Thoughts

Meditations

Thoughts

Meditations

Enrich

Our lives are enriched by
what we hold in our hearts
Not
What we hold in our hands....

Thoughts

Date

Meditations

Thoughts

Meditations

Bitter

Bitter is the fruit that does not get enough sun.
It clings to the tree afraid to release...
Shuddering as the apple is plucked nearby
Its seed will never rest in the earth and multiply.

Thoughts

Date

Meditations

Thoughts

Meditations

On Love

Love is such a relative term/word
It can crumble in the wake of the slightest tremor and
for some it can stand impenetrable in the
strongest of winds.
It is the latter I will embrace....
I have so much love to give and so much to receive
There is no loss to me for him who
cannot withstand a tremor.
I seek to stand in the shelter of the arms of
the one who can withstand the wind
I love strong and hard…unshakable, immovable, and
impenetrable…always
I must be loved ..Unshakable, immovable,
impenetrable…always...

Thoughts

Meditations

Thoughts

Date

Meditations

Painful Outcome

If in the face of pain
You seek solace in a sulking silence.
It is louder than a symphony
and
thus becomes your soliloquy.

Thoughts

Date

Meditations

Thoughts

Date

Meditations

Tribute

To my dear readers,

May you embark on a transformative journey, From
the place of "No Longer" to the realm of "Not Yet."

May you discover the power within you, unveiling the
brilliance of Your Essential Self.

May this book guide you towards a resounding "YES,"
a resolute affirmation of your authentic being.

May you find courage amidst uncertainty, and embrace
the unknown with unwavering trust.

To my cherished family,

You have been my rock and my guiding light, support-
ing me through every twist and turn.

This dedication is a tribute to your unwavering love, for
it is your encouragement that fuels my spirit.

May you also find your own YES, and be inspired to
live your most meaningful lives.

To my loyal friends,

You have stood by my side, unwaveringly, through
moments of triumph and tribulation.

This dedication is a testament to our bond, for it is your
presence that lifts me higher.

May you too uncover your Essential Self, and forge a
path of authenticity and fulfillment.

Together, let us embrace the journey,
Between "No Longer" and "Not Yet,"

As we discover the profound beauty of our YES.

With Love, Admiration & Appreciation
Nea Anna Simone

About The Author

Nea Anna Simone has captured the hearts of readers across the globe. Her works have resonated deeply with audiences, earning her the esteemed title of New York Times Bestselling Author.

From the moment Nea Anna Simone burst onto the literary scene with her debut novel, "Reaching Back," from the Mignon Samuels Trilogy her unique voice and captivating narratives have garnered widespread critical acclaim. The book swiftly soared to the top of national Bestseller lists, enchanting readers with its poignant exploration of love, loss, and the resilience of the human spirit. Its success marked the beginning of a brilliant literary career.

Following the triumph of "Reaching Back," Nea Anna Simone further solidified her place among the literary elite with her second novel, "Reborn." The second installment of her celebrated Mignon Samuels trilogy continued to captivate readers, delving even deeper into the complexities of the human experience. The depth of emotion and intricate character development within its pages cemented its position on the prestigious New York Times Bestseller list.

The trilogy was flawlessly concluded with "The Substance of Things," the final masterpiece that brought Nea Anna Simone's vision to its breathtaking culmination. This concluding work served as a testament to her profound storytelling ability, leaving readers spell- bound and thirsting for more. Her ability to touch the hearts and minds of individuals from diverse cultures is a testament to the universality of her themes and the power of her words.

Books By The Author

Discover more captivating stories from the author:

MIGNON SAMUELS TRILOGY
Reaching Back: Immerse yourself in a gripping tale of love, loss, and self-discovery as the characters navigate the depths of their past and find hope for the future.

Reborn: Experience a mesmerizing story filled with mystery, and unexpected twists. Delve into a world where ordinary lives collide with extraordinary destinies. Uncover hidden truths and embark on a transformative journey that will leave you breathless.

The Substance of Things: Prepare for the breathtaking finale of the trilogy. Brace yourself for a profound literary experience.

Available in bookstores and on-line retailers.

www.neasimone.com

For special appearances, book club requests, or autographed copies, please contact Nea Simone at **info@neasimone.com**.

Contact the author and delve deeper into the enchanting worlds she creates. Don't miss out on the opportunity to engage with Nea Simone and bring her extraordinary stories to life.